Tarnished Treasures

by Michael Barrett

Copyright © 2024 by – Michael Barrett – All Rights Reserved.

It is not legal to reproduce, duplicate, or transmit any part of this document in either electronic means or printed format. Recording of this publication is strictly prohibited.

Table of Contents

Dedication i
About the Author ii
FOR MOTHER 1
4 am TREES 2
DARKNESS UNTOLD 3
MELLOW MELANCHOLY 4
ABOUT ME 5
HOLLOW EYES 6
SEEN IN THE DARK 7
SOMETHING MORE 8
I HOPE 10
JAZZ MUSICIAN 11
WE LISTENED TO THE MUSIC 12
LAVA LAMP 13
THE SONG OF THE SHORE 14
THE MELODY MAN AND HIS LUTE 16
THE WOODCUTTER'S DAUGHTER 17
OLD-FASHIONED FIREPLACE 19
BASHFUL AUTUMN MOON 20
SADNESS 21
A SINGLE TEAR IN THE RAIN 22
A NOTE UNREAD 23
STOPPED CLOCK 25
BY HEART 26
WHITE HORSES 28
INSPIRATION 29

BY THE STILL WATERS	30
WHEN THE WORLD IS ASLEEP	31
ONE NIGHT ATOP THE CLIFFS	33
CITY OF BRISTOL BLUES	35
CASCADE STEPS	36
LONG AND WINDING HILL	37
OLD STONE WALL	38
POET OF THE CITY	39
SPIRITUAL LAMENTS	40
REMORSE	41
INNER BEAUTY	42
THE POND	43
CLOUDS	44
COOKING	46
THE GARDENER	47
PERRANPORTH ROMANCE	48
EARTH ANGEL	50
LADY OF THE DREAM	51
SILENCE OF THE NIGHT	52
OUR MISTRESS	53
FOR NO ONE ELSE	54
ICE PATCHES	55
LOST	56
UPON THE SANDS	58
DEATHLY SLEEP	59
TRAVELLING ROAD	61

Dedication

For my wife, Twané
Who made me a better man
I thank you always

About the Author

Michael grew up in the amazing city of Bristol, England, but found himself most at ease when exploring the amazing views of the Mendip Hills and lush trails of New Forest National Park. Some of his fondest memories are from spending time amongst the ancient ruins and castles of the Brecons of South Wales. While travelling through the awe-inspiring countryside, a deep love for writing and music became a form of expression and solace; in turn, this helped him overcome the difficult struggles that he faced as a youth.

After spending some time in the exotic beauty of South Africa, Michael fell in love twice, first with the breathtaking oceanic coastline of the Western Cape and then with his future wife to whom this book is dedicated.

Now, Michael lives with his wife and children in Ireland, which has come to evoke yet more joy and awe in the beauty and splendour of his God, who created such a beautiful home for the inspiration of all mankind.

FOR MOTHER

I recall when I was young,
How we would dance all night long
To the music as it played
While your husband was away.
We would sit for hours to chat,
All those many years far back;
Dim-lit room as candles burned,
'til the time your man returned.

Purple cloaked sky
The silence broken by trees
Howling at the wind

DARKNESS UNTOLD

There's a darkness untold
Yet I fight ever bold.
I search, but cannot see
The unfortunate fate that is yet to be.

As I stumble in life
With my dreams full of strife,
I live, but remain dead,
For I fear that this world is just in my head.

I try harder yet again
But my hopes are in vain.
I grasp while pressures bound
Imprisoning my heart in tombs underground

I shudder at the rain
That gives me grief and pain.
I feel, but emotions flee,
So inexplicable and unreal to me.

There was darkness untold,
Yet I fought ever bold.
I searched but never could see
That unfortunate fate impending on me.

MELLOW MELANCHOLY

You fill me with melancholy
      but it feels a touch mellow,
Kind of like grey but yellow.

You fill me with resentment
      but it feels far from uncouth,
Kind of like lies but truth.

You fill me with lonely sadness
      but it feels so warm and bright,
Kind of like wrong but right.

You fill me with such pain and hate
      but it feels as soft as wool,
Kind of like empty but full.

You fill me with turbulence
      but it feels tranquil and calm,
Kind of like wounds without harm.

You fill me with distorted thoughts
      but it feels so full of chaste,
Kind of like loosed but embraced.

You fill me with sinister gloom
      but it feels like the purest air,
Kind of like the foul and fair.

ABOUT ME

I feel me
I see me
I hear me
I smell me
I taste me
I sense me

I love me
I hate me
I loathe me
I adore me
I hit me
I kick me

I heal me
I have me
I lose me
I find me
I am me

But I do not know me

HOLLOW EYES

The tension grows inside,
My mind's been scarred by this feeling.
From such a small ember
There are now burns on the ceiling.
Debris on the floorboards
Shrouded by the soot and ash;
I never saw the fire
Until I felt my structure crash.

I still hear the laughter
And the voices from behind me,
With no choice but to go on
And to continue blindly.
It's just an illusion,
Although the jeering seems so real,
Constant mental anguish
Is all my faded soul can feel.

A collection of thoughts
Causing angst with the abrasion,
Lateral and illogic,
Not fitting with the equation.
Perception becomes lost
Through paranoid eyes of hollow;
A thought once entertained
Is a hard thing not to follow.

SEEN IN THE DARK

In blood so thick that bubbles black
I see many hearts beat so slack;
Through strange news days, our lives are stained,
With wise words lost and so few gained.

Desireless lives so loveless lie
Within their sorrow drifting by.
Tears are found only to be lost,
Running away with an unknown cost.

Night does rise to kill lights' pleasures
From the home of tarnished treasures.
In cursed lands around us see
Happiness slain by misery.

In folding's of a worn-out age
Forever through foolish battles wage,
Lasting hope but is never filled
Have made men die and others killed.

Through blood so black that bubbles thick
Man's greedy nature spreads too quick;
Within our lives are times so stained,
With wise words lost, and sadness gained.

SOMETHING MORE

As the light on a Winter's day
Ever carelessly is fleeting,
So, too, my gently hurting heart
Is shamefully retreating;
To be replaced with love so warm
Darkened days, no more repeating.
My soul hopes for the peace that's sure
For something more...
    For something more...

As showers on a Springtime eve
Rain down to flow into the drain,
So, too, I know this falling faith
Will wash away for strength regained;
And though it still may sometimes hurt
My heart will beat with trust again.
My soul yearns for a spiritual cure
For something more...
    For something more...

As the sun on a Summer morn
Has scorched the valley plains bone dry,
So, too, my fear has boiled and burned
From this bittersweet lullaby,
And If I sing it every day
I have the will to get me by.
My soul searches through every pore;
For something more...
    For something more...

As the dusk on an Autumn's night
Blows away the decay of leaves,
So, too, this love has pained and past
To become the dust of the breeze;
With every season coming and gone
I feel my heartache gently ease.
My soul still cries for what is pure;
For something more…
For something more…

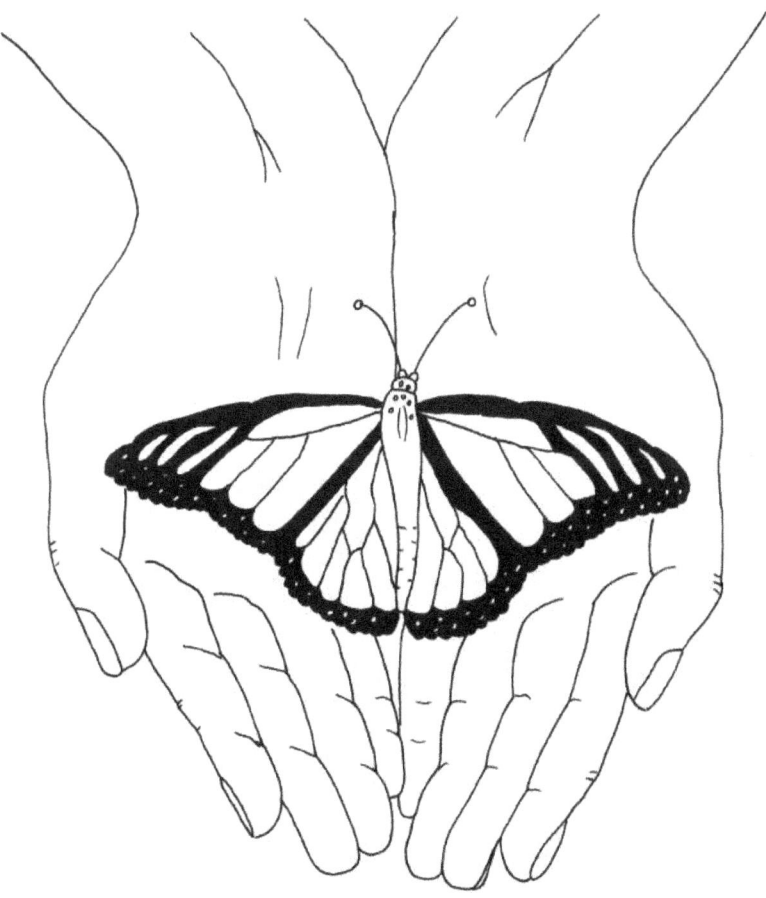

I HOPE

I hope

This is all just

Me growing up.

That I may actually

One day

find

What it is

I'm growing up for

I hope.

Moonlight spotlight
Jazz musician plays
Brass horn and lungs

WE LISTENED TO THE MUSIC

We listened to the music
Of the soundtrack to our lives,
Winging across the eternal blue
To wherever time may fly.

We listened to the rock-stars,
Fell in and out of love.
We grew up in the summer
And learned about our God.

We listened to the silence
In nostalgic autumn nights,
Memories whispered by the rain
Within its soft decline.

We listened to the heartbeat
Of the path that is our own,
As we fly away from childhood
To where our dreams may roam.

We listened to the ages
All in the music flow,
Winging across the eternal blue
To wherever time will go.

LAVA LAMP

Colours transcendental,
Music instrumental,
The room is gently rocking.
Lava lamp in twilight
Weaving through the skylight,
From where the rooks are flocking.

Colours instrumental,
Music transcendental,
The room is softly sinking.
Lava lamp in midnight
Seething through the starlight,
Where distant worlds are shrinking.

THE SONG OF THE SHORE

I sit 'pon a throne of white sand,
On the shore of timeless space
With the sun, a golden apple,
Setting in the eyes of my face.
Bright crystals dance on the ocean –
Silent - in dusky aura grace.

Celestial clouds circled over
The crystal calmness of my mind;
In front of me stretched an ocean
With a troubled past far behind.
Gold hangs like temples in the sky
Where stars take their seats in kind.

The sun spills like a sleeping rose
Nodding its head for deep slumber,
I dream of what has passed this day
For time and space, laze in wonder.
Soon, the world will glide in starlight
As I sit in muse and ponder.

Darkness sweeps like a pale shadow
In the bejewelled fading sky,
Starlight dreams are born from these waves
Of the ocean before my eye.
They give birth to the dusk that heaves
With her glossy, pearlescent sigh.

The shingles of the scalloped sand
Reflect the portrait of the moon,
I know the sky spreads forever
But it seems to unfold too soon.
As I turn home, the shore remains
Breathing the singing of her tune.

THE MELODY MAN AND HIS LUTE

Deep within the forest,
Beneath exotic fruit,
See the Melody Man
Playing upon his lute.

High upon the branches,
The song-birds sing along,
Their throats reach the right notes
Never to get one wrong.

His songs soothe the life-stream,
But no one hears him play,
As he strums throughout the night
And deep into the day

The grass dances along,
With the harmonising breeze,
His tunes flow in rhythm
Through the swaying of the trees.

Bluebells kiss his fingers
And Violas hug his toes,
As hues of blue and green
Blend as the daylight grows.

Deep within existence,
Whenever the Earth is mute,
Hear the hymn of the Melody Man
Playing upon his lute.

THE WOODCUTTER'S DAUGHTER

Far off in a land long ago
In a valley between two seas,
A cottage stood shrouded by grass
And the branches of tall trees.
There, within a woodcutter lived
With a daughter of gentlest hands.
They said she was the prettiest
And fairest girl in all the land.

The moon hangs high, the stars shine bright,
Her love will come with the midnight.

She donned herself with a red hood
And proceeded to creep outside,
Her true love came from a distance
Upon a river-raft and tide.
His hair was dark, and skin was tanned
And in his eyes were stars and moons.
He took her hand and led her to
A cave by the silent lagoon.

The moon was fat, the night in depth,
They kissed alone, her father slept.

He lay her by the ravine side
And revealed his heart internal
By singing her songs all night long
Of his love for her eternal.
He took her home and bade farewell
Through the window bay once more, they kissed.
Her father woke and knew not of
His daughter and her lover's tryst.

The moon had set, her love was gone
He'll return with the setting sun.

OLD-FASHIONED FIREPLACE

The shadows dance within the flames
In an old-fashioned fireplace,
The carven images in the frames
Enjoy it with their grinning face.
The fire crackled and whispered our names
As the shadows jumped into the empty space
Behind where we sat to play secret games
Then, they returned to their old-fashioned fireplace.

Bashful autumn moon
Held on the fingertips of trees
Tracing for your heart

SADNESS

I watched you walk away,
Your beauty left my sight,
Remembering when our laughter
Turned into a horrible fight.
As you turned around to leave,
I felt my heart begin to brace,
There was sadness in your tears
But a smile across your face.

We spent that night together,
Before it all fell apart,
And as I held your body close
I thought you held me in your heart.
How did things go so wrong?
I guess I'll never know.
There's that smile upon your lips
But a sadness that you show.

Now, here I am alone,
Dreaming of your face,
So hard to forget
And impossible to replace.
I wonder where you are.
I wonder who's with you.
Will you ever think of us?
Did you feel the sadness, too?

A SINGLE TEAR IN THE RAIN

The sun is setting slothfully
Behind sheets of falling rain,
I'm sure every drop is different
But to me, they look the same.
The day soon turns into the night
As the sun dies out of sight.

Your reflection isn't showing
Though the waters are all clear,
But still, I dirtied the river
With one gently fallen tear.
Now the bench where we sat decays
Abandoned to the passing days.

My soul is longing for the kiss
I once caught from your sweet lips,
And on your fading photograph
The evening rain-drop drips.
And I am finally alone
Now, your heart's no longer my home.

A NOTE UNREAD

Isn't it ironic?
How I held the letter with my forefinger and thumb,
Dabbing the opposite corner
Of the page into the naked dancing flames
Of a scented candle?

The letter not from you to me,
But from me to you.
At least, that was my intention.
I tried to seal it in a dark envelope
But my tongue was dry;
Just a petty excuse.

In it, I concealed many things,
Apologies for something,
I'm not sure I ever knew exactly what for;
A revelation, my greatest secret,
The immortal words 'I love you'.
Many of the lines were bitter and heart-breaking
Yet others were sweet and comforting;
Many times, I repeated myself
Like a broken record player.

Nothing in the letter made much sense,
So very confusing
(Including the line 'I love you'),
Like the written prose of Shakespeare's play
Spoken in poetry
By an amateur.

As the letter burns, I think of you,
Of what you may be doing right now…
Wondering if you're smiling or frowning,
Laughing or crying, Or maybe a bit of all.

I sit in darkness,
The candlestick my only source of light
Burning up my letter.
No, sorry. Your letter,
In my possession.
I become devoid of thought and feelings,
Except for those I hold for you.
The flickering of the candle
Are as a mere blur of a distant world
As I focus on the image of you
Dancing before the eyes of my mind.

Staring into the dark, thinking of you,
The burning letter lashes at my forefinger and thumb,
I'm forced to drop the ashes of the epistle
Onto the cold floor where it decays.
Although it's gone, those words still flicker and dance:
'I love you'.

But still,
Isn't it ironic?
How I held the letter with my forefinger and thumb,
Dabbing the opposite corner
Of the letter into the naked dancing
Flames…

STOPPED CLOCK

My love has gone,
My heart bereft
And pulse has stopped
At the time, she left.

With sodden eyes
She slammed the door,
The clock that hung
Then fell to the floor.,

The hands won't move,
The plastics cracked,
Despite all this
I put it back.

Ever since then
The years gone by,
I've kept the clock
But not sure why.

Sometimes I look
At this clock of mine.
Forgot that it stopped
Still shows the right time.

BY HEART

Should the stars of the sky
Disappear,
Then you will know by heart,
I have taken them for you.

Should the waves of the sea
Retreat
At your feet
And you will feel the foam gently kiss your toes,
Then you will know by heart,
Each and every kiss
Will be inspired by my love
For you.

Should your heart
Ever ache
With the pains of the world,
The troubles of life,
Or just the remembrance of a lost love,
Then you will know by heart,
That I am aching with you;
Always feeling your soul.

Should the sun
Ever waste away,
Exploding without a sound,
Then you will know by heart,
I will be here
Waiting for you,
Though I am just a boy
Falling in love with a woman,
As the stars cascade.

Should your name
Appear
Within the sand,
As if by Midas' touch,
Then you will know by heart,
Every couple that walks
Arms linked,
Hearts linked,
Across the shore
Will immediately know your name
And the love I hold, cherished,
For you.

Should I ever get the chance
To kiss you,
Then you will know my heart,
And how much you mean
To me,
By heart.

Above falling leaves
Endless ocean of azure
White horses cascade

INSPIRATION

Ink is pulsing throughout my veins,
To seep into the page
And releasing from captivity,
My feelings from their cage.

Even when the words cannot flow,
There're inspired songs among
The rhythm of the birds and beasts,
That thrives in nature's throng.

Beneath the shadowed forest boughs,
I rest on benches that
Are carved by the travelling wind,
Where centuries have sat.

By always taking paths unpaved,
I find the verse to write
Of nature or of love and loss,
While dusk drips into night.

The sky paints a new nebula,
As it spills off her brush
And splash onto the words I weave,
That makes the evening blush.

BY THE STILL WATERS

By the still waters
There stands a bird
With a beak of yellow gold,
And from within the stream
The bird sings and bathes
In synthetic water flow.

Her eyes shone with bronze
As she rests beside
Crystal fountains of silver moon,
And from within the stream
The night casts a wave
Of ripples of light of you.

By the still waters
We sat, and we played
And laid ourselves together,
From within the stream
The bird watches us kiss
By the still waters.

WHEN THE WORLD IS ASLEEP

The world is perfect.

Here, on my own,
Surrounded by trees,
And an interweaving breeze
I just sit
And feel the planet
Wax and wane.

The sound of a cool trickling stream
Makes me wonder how far she's going;
Over the shingles and far away,
A journey over numerous days,
And I just watch her drift by.

No one else can hear this sound.
No one else can see me now.
Alone but not lonely, am I.

I gaze up to a dewless sky
Reflecting the light of my eyes
In her endless body.

Dusk is my partner.
I know that she loves me,
Listening to all my joys and my pain.
She knows every corner
Of my spirit and my heart,
But never once have I told her my name.

The birds sing me songs.
The trees whisper secrets to me.
The Earth welcomes my coming
With wide-open arms.
The stars all look down
Upon my resting abode.
They've read all the poetry
Inscribed on my heart.

Cocooned in my spirit,
Free from the outside,
I embrace nature,
The most perfect of worlds.

ONE NIGHT ATOP THE CLIFFS

You stand atop the cliff.
Over the edge you gaze;
Nothing but a dark ocean,
Fading into the distance.
The wind is gently growing
And it runs along your back.
Your hair flows ahead of your face.
The waves of the water
Reflects the pools within your eyes.
Feathers of birds
Flock behind you,
Above a shadowed vale.
The masking sky falls off,
And with it, a chill
As clouds gallop at the horizon.
You stand alone.
The wind wraps around your legs,
And from the spray
Of waves beneath
A few tiny droplets
Tenderly touch your skin
Upon your naked arms and
Unsheathed face.
The darkened sky rumbles,
Where the hills disappear.
The cliff stands high,
And you sigh atop the rock.
The water seems to ebb...
The sky is dark...
A breeze blows...

The currents twist
Against your face;
A blaze across the sky like fire,
A ruby blood-red star.
The waves crash into the sky
Eyes burning like the sun
Your arms unfurl.
Your hair pushed back.
Clothes dance upon your body.
Lightning trails kindle the sky.
Warm winds lift your fingers
Until they are above your head.
Power surges through your body.
Excitement, anxiety,
Rushing through your veins.
A tingle creeps across your skin
A roar erupts like volcanic ash
Flies upon the air.
The hills rush into you
With fingertips of an unseen force,
The power kisses and caresses you
Heart ablaze with life and awe;
And you are one with the wind,
And you are one with the sky,
And you are one with the waves,
And you are one with the cliffs,
And you are one.

CITY OF BRISTOL BLUES

Plain-Jane student in her own world;
Weighed-down mother, holding her girl;
Teens on skateboards rolling around,
Jump in the air, fall to the ground;
Goths just sitting lost in their blues;
Staggering drunks drowning in booze;
Ill-struck seagulls harbour-side fly;
Together, alone, we cry.

Busking musicians play on streets;
Business-man suit, shuffles his feet;
Dreaming poet riddled with curse,
Rip out a page, write a new verse;
Foreign pilgrim stumbling for truth;
Smoking teen-child wandered since youth;
Homeless ones wake but don't know why;
Together, alone, we sigh.

Dogs all shaggy shivering cold;
Loveless mother, young but looks old;
Heart-broken girl sobbing at home,
Slumps to the floor, hangs up the phone.
Happy people drift before us,
Others depressed lost in chorus.
Life grows harder as days go by
But together, alone, we try.

CASCADE STEPS

I watched two lovers neck and kiss
In the world that became their own,
And the water slips down the steps
Into its sequined river home.

Flowing under Electric light
Over golden strips of concrete,
Echoes of fossilised footsteps
Reverberating on the street.

The inner-city hustle hides
A paradise in but one sound,
Simple trickles of waterfalls
Forming freely from out the ground.

A refraction from off the steps
Is but the stars of a light caught,
Reflecting in my peering eyes
A mirror of the starlight sort.

The breeze blew a silent whisper
With her words lost in translation,
This trickle of water serene
Language of imagination.

The boats slowly swayed in the dock
Their belonging and harboured place,
As over steps, the water falls
Timed in eternal cycle space.

LONG AND WINDING HILL

Moss and rocky road,
Leading my way to where
      I'm craving.
Wet and slippery street,
Resting in the abode
      Of summer.

Green and cracking lane,
Deserted of the cars marks
      And lashings.
Old and worn crescent,
Pebble-paved and plain
      Old-fashioned.

Long and winding hill,
Watching her house
      I stand.
If things were different,
I would love her still
      If I could.

On an old stone wall
Through car headlights at midnight
The slug trails appear

POET OF THE CITY

I find myself
      outside the committee,
           a poppy on an empty street,
A poet within a city.

I'm drawn away
      by imagination,
           a dark star in the morning light,
A man dying of frustration.

I've come undone
      inside dreams of madness,
           a romantic fool without love,
A painted clown lost in sadness.

I fly so low
      within a darkened room,
           a glimmer in a fragile mind,
A living man within a tomb.

I find myself
      trekking through my pity,
           a sharp breeze of a stagnant sky,
A poet within this city.

SPIRITUAL LAMENTS

My righteous ways are wearing thin
I'm nothing but a slave to sin.
My faith slips backwards out of sight
As it fades into scarlet night.
A battle 'twixt my mind and flesh
Succumbing to what offers death.
My soul is frozen where I stand still
But dragged through time against my will.
Lay me down for the birds to feed
Let my errors become their seed.
Sip the wine of the tears I've cried
Spiritual laments burn deep inside.

REMORSE

Sometimes, we say things
That we never wanted,
But we've said them all the same.
Sometimes, we do things
And we never planned it,
But we hold them to our name.

INNER BEAUTY

Fabricated jewels
On the outer layer of the skin,
Are just an illusion
And hide what's deep within.

The graves of our fathers,
Covered with marble and stones,
Yet all that they possess
Are dust and dead men's bones.

Eyes deceive what is seen
Like the cover of a book,
They turn blind eyes away
From where we all should look.

Beauty on the inside
Is always there forever,
But that which is outside
May be gone whenever.

Like the ugly duckling,
Some have beauty that's asleep
And when they get older
It sprouts for them to keep.

THE POND

The dusty galaxy
Before our simple eyes,
Shimmers with small ripples
Beyond our pale-blue skies.

It is but a small pond,
A simple lake of dew,
A pool with different shades
All mixed in a navy hue.

Planets swim like fishes
Around the blazing boat,
Of the bright golden Sun
Animate and afloat.

In the hidden boathouse,
The Pond-Keeper and his son,
Reflect upon the ripples
Their perfect creation.

CLOUDS

It's hard for us to be
Ever so pristine,
It's hard to be perfect
When we're so unclean,
It's hard to be so warm
When we feel so blue,
It's hard to see the sky
When there are clouds in view.

It's hard to shoot the moon
When we have no aim,
It's hard to keep alive
If we have no name,
It's hard for us to see
An easy way through,
It's hard to see the sky
When there are clouds in view.

It's hard for us to smile
When lips crack with age,
It's hard for us to breathe
When colours turn grey,
It's hard to be as one
When we've come unglued,
It's hard to see the sky
When there are clouds in view.

It's hard to touch the stars
When we're down so low,
It's hard to carry on
When there is no flow,
It's hard to live my life
When I'm not with you,
It's hard to see the sky
When there are clouds in view.

Every raindrop that falls
Will they not dry up?
Can I please have a heart?
Unscathed and uncut?
It's hard to see the sky.
When there are clouds in view,
But I know there is hope;
I can make it through.

Standing by the pot
Herbs and spices in the stew
You fill my heart

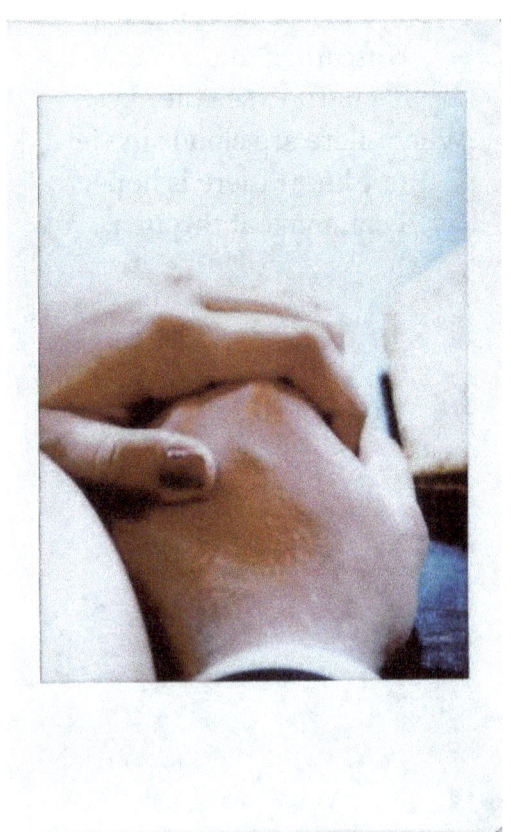

THE GARDENER

If I myself was a gardener
Not roses would I sow,
Nor daisies or sweet daffodils
Or lilies for which to grow;
In fact, I won't plant seeds that could
Be eaten or trampled too,
I would cultivate kisses
And I'd plant them all on you.

PERRANPORTH ROMANCE

Golden rays from your golden hair,
Sun-kissed freckles on skin so fair,
Running through the waves, embraced you.
The ocean swayed with turquoise dance,
Mystic aura of light entrance,
Flowing on the breeze that kissed you.

Opal beads slipping through your hand,
Pour reds and golds onto the sand,
Blending with the grains beneath you.
The ocean sprayed with mist and steam,
Backdrop beauty, a tranquil dream,
Twisting in the air around you.

Ruby clouds burn behind your smiles,
Water drifting for endless miles,
Hazing with the sky behind you.
The ocean lay with serene sheets,
Quilted softness of calm it keeps,
Prying just to be inside you.

Diamond light flickers in your eyes,
In slow motion, they tantalise,
Showing ancient worlds within you.
The ocean prayed with gentle roars,
Love-felt lashings against the shores,
Begging for the chance to hold you.

Golden light from your golden hair,
Sun-kissed lover just hiding there,
Running to my arms, embraced you.
The ocean swayed with sapphire dance,
Mystic aura of love enhance,
Flowing through our lips, I kissed you.

EARTH ANGEL

I met an angel,
Beautiful was the dame,
She had topaz eyes
And Twané was her name.

She had no halo,
No white gown and no harp,
But only a touch
That kindled my heart.

Ribbons crown her brow,
Made of opals and lace,
Eyes of diamond light
And a celestial face.

She had ruby lips,
And flesh of porcelain,
And a black nightdress
Dripped from her tender skin.

Flowers in her hair
Put perfume in her kiss,
No other pleasures
Could ever rival this.

I met an angel,
Beautiful and divine,
Making me happy
Just to know she is mine.

LADY OF THE DREAM

If I could only take you in my arms
To hold you O' so tight,
And we'll lie as the darkness ensues
Until the morning light.
O' how I yearn to taste your velvet kiss
Ease away my pains,
As I feel your beloved beating heart
Pulsating through my veins.
You heat me up with gentle, burning lips
So hot I melt and steam,
If I could only take you in my arms
O' lady of the dream.

If I could only move the stars for you
To make them spell your name,
And we'll watch them sparkle like fireflies
Until the morning came.
O' how I yearn to watch the tide with you
Washing away the day,
As the golden sun goes softly setting
All in her silent way.
You fill me up with the breath of your love
So much I want to scream,
If I could only move the stars for you
My lady of the dream.

SILENCE OF THE NIGHT

In a room of fragrance and scent,
Our bodies longed to mingle.
Within our dreams, a dream was dreamt.
With feelings of touch and tingle.

Down from the sky, the moonlight shined,
The candle's breath was showing
And in our heart, soul, and mind.
Passion came wreathing and flowing.

Our lips so hot they melt the air,
Our bodies entwined as one.
My fingers fair, caress your hair,
The bondage of time is undone.

Warm breath cut through the silent night,
Filled the room with feelings, serene
Of tingles that touched the twilight
To the spaces of you and me between.

OUR MISTRESS

In the softness of gentle night,
Our mistress dons a cloak of light –
An aura of her face of pearl –
Her glowing veil and mask unfurl.
She whispers words for pain to ease,
She blows a kiss, a midnight breeze.
A bejewelled rune in space she lies –
Within the dark, she'll hypnotize.
An orb of grace we sit below,
The night stands still as time breathes slow.
If I could pluck her from her throne,
To you, I give this splendent stone.
Her dust of sparks around us twist,
Pulls us close to share our kiss
A witness to our love so bold.
A bond with her, we have to hold.
Forever comes, and dawn arrives,
Another day within our lives.
We leave behind the one we share,
Until her light illumes the air.
In pleasantness of blooming day
Our mistress sleeps and slips away –
An ancient rune, a symbol of
Our night, our time, as One in love.

FOR NO ONE ELSE

There's poetry flowing from my lips,
Never to reach the page
For no one else's ears but yours.

In my arms or in my heart,
You're with me constantly,
My words are always with you…

And if I could
I would tell them to the stars,
To have them whisper the words

Throughout the ebbing of the night
And from where they hide in the day
For no one else's ears but yours.

The shifting shadows
Holding onto ice patches
Not much longer now

LOST

I'm looking for a way
To stop me from feeling lost,
Taking me back to the time
'fore the path of my footsteps crossed.

I'm looking for a love
That makes my heart complete,
The kind, surpassing feelings,
That changes the bitter to the sweet.

I'm looking for a calm,
An everlasting friend,
Like those who sat by my side
As if those days would never end.

I'm looking for the form
The mirror used to see,
'fore the smoke fogged up the glass
When a younger man looked back at me.

I'm looking for a cure,
A healing to the bones,
To restore to me my strength
And bring back the skipping of the stones.

I'm looking for the youth,
The bloom that flew so fast,
When any choice seemed so right
And I thought those nights would always last.

I'm looking for something,
Whatever it may be,
So I can find myself again
If there is no one searching for me.

I'm looking for a life
To build my world upon,
Whether I am lost or found,
I must be proud of who I've become.

UPON THE SANDS

A setting sun, a burning oil-painting
Above the delicate gossamer ocean,
The gentle roar, a passionate moan.

Echoes of children once at play,
Whispers fade into the wind,
A few hermit shells – now empty,
A bottle or two here and there,
Tresses of abandoned seaweed,
A lonely flower – deserted,
A gull atop silver stones,
Crabs and starfish bathing together,
Oceanic husks embedded like sequins,
Endless grains of a golden dress,

And two sets of footsteps
Dropping and drifting off
Into the honey-glazed horizon.

DEATHLY SLEEP

Into the flowing ripples
Of the crystal lake, I gaze.
Around me is our valley
Where we spent so many days.

Now that you've gone
I get lonely, and I curse.
It can't get any better
Though it can't get any worse.

I cried on the dark hill
Beneath the great black oak,
As I said goodbye to you
On my tears to choke.

Since you went away
I've considered life a loss,
And I sail through life
With no ocean to cross.

You gave me treasures
That could not be found on Earth,
But without saying a word
You stole away my mirth.

Far from this icy world
You rest without fears,
But you don't even know
You've caused so many tears.

I stare into the setting sun
Sitting on a single stone.
My eyes leak slow tears
And my heart lets out a moan.

That night, the stars burned quietly
In the far-off distant space,
But their light could not compare
To your once-shining face.

All of our memories
Are in my heart to keep.
I miss you ever so much
As you lie in deathly sleep.

TRAVELLING ROAD

Stumbling along the tumbling sun,
The wind is chasing by.
Searching oceans and land beyond,
The birds so freely fly.

The trees evoke a sense of hope,
Following the highway.
Wandering clouds and stars elope,
Bring an end to the day.

Travelling road the path in flow,
The streetlights guide me through.
Summons me where my heart must go,
And leading me to you...

Calling me home.

AUTHOR'S NOTE

First of all, I am truly grateful that you have chosen to read this book. This is a small selection of poems that I have written throughout my life; the first at the tumultuous age of 14 and the most recent at nearly 40. I hope that as you read this collection you have found an affinity with at least some of them, whatever you are currently going through whether times of sadness, heartache, love or joy, thank you for giving me the chance to share my experiences with you. At times, my challenges seemed insurmountable, but I got through them. So will you and you will be stronger for it. Those in your life right now may not be tomorrow so remember to cherish those who are precious and choose carefully those to whom you entrust your heart.

I would like to thank Chris Thomas with whom I first shared my poetry. Among many things he encouraged me to see that the first draft is rarely the final and not to give up on writing. He helped me more than he may be aware of.

I would like to send my love and thanks to my family; my parents in the UK especially gifted me to find beauty in all things and I will always appreciate that they introduced me to good music. To my beautiful wife who assisted my healing, restoring my faith in love and showing me that I am, as we all are, deserving of that precious commodity. My amazing children she gave me have provided a happiness that I never thought possible.

I would also like to thank my publishing team for all their hard work. Their tireless efforts have made this book a reality.

Lastly, but most importantly; for the world we have around us I can only thank my God whose name is Jehovah, the creator of this beautiful planet that we call home and our wonderful imagination. I only came to know Him later in life though and so no matter what your personal belief may be, dear reader, I'm sure you agree that the natural wonders adorning our planet are truly awe-inspiring and worthy of praise.

www.ingramcontent.com/pod-product-compliance
Lightning Source LLC
Chambersburg PA
CBHW052206110526
44591CB00012B/2104